INSPIRING TRUE STORIES BOOK FOR 5 YEAR OLD GIRLS!

I am 5 and Amazing

Inspiring True Stories of Courage, Self-Esteem, Self-Love, and self-Confidence

Paula Collins.

Contents

Introduction

Hello! Do you realize how amazing you are?

You are exceptional. You are completely unique. Always remember that! You are the only you there is in the entire world, and that's out of billions of people!

The world has many big and small hurdles in store for you. Sometimes you might think that you can't make it. You might get very scared or doubt yourself. However, I want to tell you a secret. Everybody feels like this from time to time! Even adults.

In this Inspiring Stories book, you will meet other amazing girls. These girls overcome their fears, show great inner strength, and reveal their bravery.

Of course, you can show all these qualities too, but you must start believing in yourself. That is exactly what this book will help you learn to do.

You can shine your light in your corner of the world and bring that light to other people when you let go of fear and keep learning lessons. When you believe in yourself, you can accomplish anything. You are an Amazing girl

Sofia's New Adventure

Have you ever been afraid, afraid of the dark, afraid of being alone, afraid of not making friends, afraid of meeting new people?

You are unique, intelligent, and wonderful; It is normal to feel fear and trepidation when faced with new situations.

Finding a way to let your creativity flow despite your fears can help you realize that just because

something is new to you doesn't mean it's bad. It just means you haven't experienced it yet; once you realize that your nerves won't hold you back, you can show the world how amazing you are.

Sophia watched from her room through the window as two children played in the park in front of her house. She remembered her friends from her old town, how she had fun with them, and they spent unforgettable moments riding bikes, playing riddles, playing ball, playing hide and seek...

Her memory stopped when her mom opened the door and said, "Sophia, have you prepared everything for tomorrow? do you have everything ready to enter your new school? your backpack? your supplies? your new notebooks? and what you are going to wear tomorrow?" asked her mom.

At that moment, Sophia remembered that tomorrow would be her first day of school in this city. She had been in her new home for almost a month now because her father had been transferred to a new city due to a promotion at the company where he worked.

Sophia was very sad to have left her friends. She missed her house, her room, and her neighborhood where she had spent happy times with her friends, and she especially missed Sara, her best friend.

Sophia answered her mom," Yes, mommy, I have everything ready. I have organized everything; I have my new shoes, I have the jacket that grandma gave me, my books are already packed in the backpack, and everything is ready, mom. I am the one who is not ready; I am very nervous, I don't know how it will be, and I don't know what to do. I'm very nervous. I don't know what tomorrow will be like."

And she continued, "I am very nervous because I don't know if tomorrow I will be alone all day since I don't know anyone, will no one talk to me, will I have lunch alone, and will I be alone at recess? Will I eat lunch alone, and will I be alone at recess?"

Her mom hugged her and said, "Sophia, don't worry, sweetheart, you are an amazing little girl, and you will see that tomorrow everything will turn out great."

Sitting on the bed, her mom adjusting her hair, told her, "I remember when it was my first day of school, I was just like you, very nervous; my heart was jumping with excitement and nerves. I remember your grandparents took me to my new school and I met Mrs. Salazar, my new teacher. There were many children with their parents too, and after Mrs. Salazar welcomed us, we entered the classroom, and I sat next to a girl named Penelope. Do you remember her? my best friend since school, I will never forget that day".

Sophia could not sleep well that night. She imagined the worst: that a boy would make fun of her, that she wouldn't find her classroom, that she would be alone all day, that no one would talk to her, that she would eat lunch alone.

Finally, she managed to fall asleep until she was interrupted by the sound of the alarm clock. It was time to get up. When she opened her eyes, she smelled the delicious smell of the pancakes her mother had prepared for breakfast.

From the kitchen, her mother called her, "Sophia, breakfast is ready; come downstairs because we are late."

"I'm coming, mom," she said, "I'm just finishing getting ready."

At that moment, Sophia began to think about what she could think of not going to school, and she felt that her heart was going to burst.

So she decided to tell her mom, "mom, I'm sick, I feel sick, and my stomach hurts. I think I won't be able to go to school today."

Mom understanding what was happening to her, went up to the room and gave her a big hug, stroked her head, and said, "don't worry, sweetheart, everything is going to be okay; you will see, it's normal to feel scared but don't worry everything is going to be okay." And she added, "you are a beautiful, wonderful, and cheerful girl. You are going to see that your teacher is going to be very kind, you are going to make friends in your new school, and you are going to be very happy."

Sophia was so anxious that she couldn't taste her mom's delicious pancakes.

Her dad also cheered her up by telling his stories about when he had been on his first day of school.

Sophia was reassured by her dad's stories realizing that she was not the only one who had been through that situation, "I can, too," She thought to herself.

Finally, her mom pulled her out of her thoughts, "Sophia, it's our turn to leave for school now. You don't want us to be a little late, sweetie."

They got into the car and started the drive to the new school. Sophia looked out the window as if looking for something or someone she knew from her old town.

When they arrived at the school, they found many children entering accompanied by their parents.

Sophia could hardly feel her legs from fear, her hands were sweating, and she could barely hold her gaze. Her mother took her by the hand and kissed her on the forehead, and said: "Sophia, it's time to meet your new school, don't worry, sweetheart, everything will be fine. Do you want me to take you by the hand? she asked.

As they were walking into the classroom, her feet stopped, and suddenly, Sophia said to her mom, "Can we come back tomorrow? I think it's okay if I don't stay today, right?

Her mother looked her in the eyes and, with a smile, said: "don't worry, trust you; everyone looks very nice, and I'm sure they will receive you very well".

At that moment, they met the teacher of the classroom, Vicky, and she said to her, "I imagine you must be Sophia".... "What a joy to meet you. We've been waiting for you", she gently stroked her head, and Sophia felt calmer.

Her parents escorted her into the living room and greeted all the children and parents present.

Sophia looked for a place to sit. Almost everyone was already occupied, and teacher Vicky asked Luna to run and open space for Sophia.

When Sophia sat down, Luna asked her: "Hi, my name is Luna. What is your name?" "Sophia." She answered in a trembling voice.

Class started, and the teacher was very kind and cheerful. She asked all the children to hold hands and form two circles, one inside the other, and each child introduced himself or herself to the child in front of him or her.

At first, Sophia felt like she was going to faint, but by the time she had introduced herself to the third child, she felt more comfortable, knowing that most of them were new children like her.

As they introduced themselves to the last child, Luna, she felt as if they already knew each other, and they continued to talk about all the things they had in common, like playing in the park, making riddles, playing hide and seek, until they heard Vicky's voice, "Sophia and Luna, we are done with introductions, you can sit down now."

After meeting her classmates, Sophia felt very relieved and confident, especially when she met Luna.

A bell rang, announcing recess. All the children ran out of the classroom. Sophia was delayed because one boy on his way out tripped over her backpack, and all her books and crayons were scattered on the floor.

After gathering her supplies and organizing her backpack, she found no one inside the classroom.

She went out to look for Luna to play with her as they had arranged, but she couldn't find her, the school was big, and she couldn't find her, nor any of her classmates.

Sophia reached the playground, where there were older children. Her legs started to shake again, she began to feel butterflies fluttering in her stomach, and suddenly a soccer ball hit her from behind.

Sophia could not hide her anguish and began to cry.

Suddenly she heard a voice calling her; it was her teacher Vicky who was holding Luna's hand.

They approached Sophia and comforted her.

Luna asked her, "What happened to you? Why are you crying? I was looking for you as we agreed, but when I couldn't find you, I asked the teacher to help me.

After Sophia calmed down, she told them what had happened to her between sobs, and her teacher hugged her, saying, "Oh poor thing, what a scare you had. Don't worry; everything is all right now." "We're here with you now." She added. Luna took her by the hand and said, "Come on, let's go play with the other children."

They went to the special green area for the little ones and started playing on the swings.

Finally, Sophia calmed down and began to smile and enjoy unforgettable moments with her new friend until the end of the day on her first day of school.

When the bell rang to leave for home, Sophia saw her mother approaching the classroom. Her mom was surprised that instead of running out to hug her, she wanted to introduce her to her new best friend, Luna.

Then, on the way home, Sophia went on and on about all the adventures of the first day of school, especially meeting Luna, a very kind and cheerful girl who had become her new best friend.

Sophia understood that many times, fear makes us see the bad in new experiences and that if we face it and manage to overcome it, we can live wonderful experiences, such as meeting new people and friends.

Sophia also understood that when fear comes, it is because new and incredible things are about to happen.

Feeling fear of the new and unknown is normal. Everyone experiences fear at one time or another, even adults. Feeling fear is not a bad thing; on the contrary, it is often a sign that new adventures are about to happen.

Show the world the wonderful girl you are, face your fears, and know that you are not alone and that you have wonderful people around you who love and support you always.

Mom's Work Day

Did you know that mom and dad are more than our parents and have things to do? Did you know that they have dreams and work to fulfill them, striving just like you do in school? This is the story of Megan, who accompanies her mother to work one day.

Megan was in her living room on the couch, watching her cell phone. She had planned to spend the day quietly, not going out. Her mother was going about her business. Lately, she had seen her very busy with some work.

Mom, who seemed to be overloaded with things, sat down next to her and looked at her with a worried air.

-I have something to tell you.

-Tell me.

-They moved up a project from my work, and I have to go today to present it. I can't leave you alone, you have to come with me because on top of that Nadia's son got sick, and she won't be able to come and take care of you.

Nadia was the nanny who took care of her when her mother was absent all day.

Megan felt annoyed, rolled her eyes, and thought that she was a big girl and that she could stay home alone. She probably wouldn't even move from the couch.

She felt that her mother was always working and that, lately, she was worse.

-I've had a lot of work these days. I promise to make it up to you when I'm done. -Her mother told her.

-I know you want to stay alone, she said, but you

can't, even though you're grown up, it's not right, so you must come with me.

Megan was upset, but she looked at her mother and read in her face that she wanted to run things well. She looked exhausted and stressed. Megan's annoyance faded, and she agreed on a good way to go with her to work. She went to get ready.

Many things began to go through her mind. What would her mom's office be like? She thought about it what her building would be like. She had never been there. She thought about the possibility that other kids her age would be there and she could go and meet them.

What would the boss be like? Would he be like those grumpy guys he sees on TV who yell at their employees? Many questions came to her mind.

When they were already in the car, Megan asked her questions, already interested in her mother:

-What color is your building?

-Brown.

-Do you have a lot of coworkers?

-Yes, quite a few, but I'm handling this project on my own because it's in my area.

-Is your boss a fighter?

-Not much; he's good.

-Do you have an office?

-Yes, it's big, you'll like it.

-Shall we go to your office?

-I'm not; you are. You'll be calm there, and you can continue on your cell phone or with my computer.

-Where will you go?

-To the boardroom. I will present the project to everyone there.

Megan thought of the boardroom as a kind of auditorium with many people inside, a red curtain at the back, and a light above her mother's head, who would nervously present whatever she was going to present.

They entered the building. In the basement, her mother left the car, and they went up the elevator.

-What is that? -Megan asked when she saw a large reception area that looked like a doctor's office.

-It's the reception for those arriving.

-Did you trick me and bring me to the doctor?

-No, said the mother after laughing, I work here.

She saw that inside that company, people were going from one side to the other. Each one passed by and greeted their mother and went on their way. This surprised Megan.

-Everyone knows you. - Said in a whisper.

-Sure, I've worked here for years. We all know each other, and we're friends.

-You're the popular girl around here, said Megan.

-Something like that. -Her mother laughed.

Megan was surprised that there were so many people out and about, going about their business in a hurry but happy as if they were busy with their jobs. Everything augured that it was a great day and that her mother was the protagonist, the one who would make it happen, and that was why she had been so stressed the last few days working so many hours.

She felt like she was in a luxurious place, as everything seemed new, technology on every desk, people sitting, lighting in every corner, air conditioning built-in, and every space with things to do.

They finally arrived at his mother's office. It was big, with a computer with a huge screen.

-What a screen you have, Mom.

-Yes, that's where I design my projects, and I need to see them well.

Her mother was an architect, using special programs to draw up plans for houses and buildings. But apparently, she had been working on something of her own for some even longer time.

Megan could be at ease in that office or follow her mother wherever she went, no problem. Although she hadn't seen another child so far, she wasn't bored. She was entertained and very curious about what her mother was doing.

From afar, she saw the boardroom, which was very different from how she had imagined it. It was an office in the middle of the whole space, made of glass. From the outside, you could see everyone, and in the center of this room, there was a table with many chairs, an acrylic blackboard, and a device that she later learned was a video beam, where they projected images to present things. That was where her mother would go.

Megan saw her mother preparing her things to go to that meeting room and thought that she was working for her dreams just like her, who sometimes imagined what she was going to be when she grew up. Her mother thought about how she could grow more professionally.

-If you want, you can come to see me, but you can't talk or interrupt, her mother told her; Megan nodded.

Mom went out to the boardroom and left her in the office; she saw that when she came in, many other people did too. They stood at the table, although her mother stood and took out a laptop where she prepared something that soon lit up on the wall. They dimmed the lights a bit, and from afar, she could see her talking as if she were giving a lecture.

Megan's curiosity got the better of her, and she went

to snoop around quietly. Soon she realized that her mother was presenting an immense project that dealt with a shopping mall. As she saw on the screen, it had many levels and looked big, and in those images, it seemed simply spectacular.

Did Mom design that all by herself? Megan thought, for it was a work of art, and she was amazed at what she could do.

Her mother gave her entire presentation, and when she finished, the others asked her questions, which she confidently answered. When she finished, everyone applauded. Mom saw her and winked at her, happy and relieved. Her presentation was a success.

When her mother returned to the office, Megan was already there with the cell phone, for she had seen the most important thing. She was happy and proud of what she had done.

-Did you design that mall by yourself? -It was the first thing she asked her.

-Yes, I have time for it. It's exhausting work but satisfying. They've approved it, and they'll start building it in a while.

-Will everyone know it's your work?

-In the papers where it says Architect will be my name, yes.

-That's incredible! -Can we go?

-Of course, when they build it, although it will take a while, it's a lot of work, but of course, we'll go. Besides, it's not far from home. It's by the park.

You were very good today, daughter; thank you for coming with me.

-You did great, Mom. I'm proud of you for doing that so beautifully.

-Shall we celebrate with ice cream?

-I think it's great.

Mother and daughter went off to celebrate the presentation of the project, and the time they spent together. They ate double-serve ice cream, as the occasion called for it.

Your parents are more than your parents. Besides taking care of us, protecting us, and being there for us, they have projects and dreams to fulfill, just like you do. If you ask them questions, you will discover wonders and unknown stories of everything they do day by day.

Weekend At The Beach

Have you ever fought with someone because they did something you didn't like? Have you ever felt that they fight with you only because they don't listen to you? Fights can arise because there is a lack of communication, either because we do not express ourselves correctly or others do not. In this story, you will discover that fights should not transcend beyond the initial and that communication is vital in our daily lives.

Amanda woke up and felt a little warmth that

foreshadowed that it would be hot that day. She looked out her window, and an orange sun was rising through the clouds. It was in the hot season, and she thought she was going to sweat a lot that day and have a bad mood because of the weather. She loved the cold, not the summer. It was a long weekend for a holiday that she didn't even know what it was about. It was just beginning. It was Saturday. At least she would spend the day resting, watching videos, and hopefully going to the mall, where there would be air conditioning.

Her mother came into the room; apparently, she had heard her wake up or move in bed.

-Good morning, daughter. You can't imagine what we are going to do today.

-Where are we going? -Asked

-To the beach!

It was 4 hours away by car, which meant that she would drive very early in the morning to go to the house of... Aunt Mia! She was very excited because she hadn't seen her for years and she lived near the beach. She was a painter and a very interesting woman, tousled, happy, smiling, and with a freedom for life that she loved.

Soon they were in the car and the trip was quick. They arrived at the aunt's house but barely passed because immediately, her mother came out with bathing suits and what was needed to go to the beach.

Mia had a daughter the same age as Amanda, 10 years old. Her name was Lily, and both were good friends and cousins. Once at the beach, the two were inseparable. They got into the water and splashed around for hours until they felt that their fingers were numb and wrinkled from playing so much.

Swimming was already boring them. They wanted to play something else, so Lily suggested playing tag, but soon they got bored. They played hide and seek with the same result.

-Why don't they build a sand castle? -proposed Mia.

They both liked the idea and got down to work. With buckets and spoons, they began to pack the sand and arrange it.

What Amanda didn't like was the texture of the sand because it got tangled in her fingers and stuck. Rough.

-Let's build a giant wall and chase each other-proposed Lily.

-I love it!

They got down to work and created a giant fortress where the two of them could practically fit.

Amanda's mother appeared with white sunscreen gel and put it on both of them their backs. They reluctantly let her do it. They just wanted to play. First, she applied it to Lily, and when she finished, she ran off to continue playing.

While she was applying to Amanda, she asked her if she had eaten or if she wanted something more than what they had brought. But Amanda only wanted to play. She didn't think about eating.

When the mother finished applying the gel, she turned around, and an impact knocked her back a couple of steps. Something hard had hit her face and seemed to have vanished all over her face.

A burning invaded her skin, but more so, her left eye seemed to be burning at that moment, as if the fire was consuming it.

-I'm sorry- said Lily, who was in front of her. She came out of nowhere-. I wanted to hit you in the chest, not in the face. Forgive me, cousin.

-Are you all right, daughter? -asked her mother.

Amanda shook her head. It was burning so much.

-I'm so sorry.

Amanda understood her cousin, but she couldn't help but be angry.

-You didn't have to throw that at me! - Amanda shouted at her, furious.

Mia, hearing her niece's shout, got up from the chair where she was contemplating the sea and went to see what was going on.

-Are you all right, niece?

-Your daughter hit me in the face and in the eye with sand.

-Let's see, I'm going to check you out.

She started to look into her eye and ran to her purse, took out a big bottle of fresh water, and uncorked it.

-Come on, tilt your head.

She began to pour water on her face with great care and love, the sand was going away. She poured it into her eye more gently, washing it completely.

-How are you? -she asked her.

-It burns, although a little less.

-Yes, you had sand. I'll tell you a secret, we are experts in this. We know how ugly sand is. Here we go.

She went to her purse and took out some drops. She asked her to open her eye and gave her a drop, which relieved her almost instantly.

-These drops will make you feel better, it's normal for the sand to get in your eyes or the saltpeter from the sea, with this we are relieved.

-Thank you, aunt.

-Why were you shouting?

-To Lily, who threw that ball of sand at me.

Mia looked at her niece and her daughter, one next to the other, one with a guilty and sorry face and the other with a pained face, a red eye, and anger.

-I see that the theme in all this is that there was a lack of communication between the two of you, said Mia.

-That's right, said Lily.

-It's normal to play with sand, though not in the face, of course.

-I'm sorry, cousin.

-It's okay. It was an accident. It's over.

-Although it's fine to play with sand, you have to do it softly and in the lower parts so that this doesn't happen, said Mia. You know what? I'm going to play, and I'll give these two intruders in my land a good shot.

Both girls looked at each other, laughed, and ran away while Mia took sand and threw it at them.

They lasted several hours playing sand bombs, the fort, the crocodile that came out of the water and they attacked it with sand, the submarine, the shark that they tried to drown, and more things that come from the imagination, all having fun.

When the mood calmed down, and Mia felt tired, she went with her sister to the shore, and the two girls stayed playing for many hours until nightfall when they returned home to eat.

Luckily, Amanda's eye had not suffered, it was red for a while longer because the sand scraped it, but with the washing and the drops, it was only a matter of time before it healed. She understood that communication is essential to connect with others and that sometimes you have to control your impulses to get angry and yell at the first moment because her cousin when she saw her mistake, asked for forgiveness and was very sorry.

They had a fabulous weekend, they ate delicious things, they went to the beach every day, playing sand balls, even on another occasion, by mistake she threw sand in her eye, but just a little bit, she washed it off quickly and it did not become a big deal.

It was one of those unforgettable weekends. They promised to get together again during the next vacation or the next long weekend.

Amanda and Lily are two cousins who love each other. The altercation with the sand became a family anecdote that they remember with humor, as they have never fought, but a sand ball taught them the value of communicating.

It's okay to play, even sometimes, with things that include a bit of daring fun, but always communicate and make the rules clear. For example, sand should never be thrown in the face or know how to do it to avoid accidents or unpleasant surprises.

Discussions can happen when a message is misunderstood. We must always learn to communicate. If we fight with someone we love, it does not mean that we will never talk again. It is only a momentary annoyance that will surely be solved by talking.

Different Rules

Have you ever thought about what it would be like to live in your house and another house? Have you noticed that each house has different rules? However, differences are not bad, and each home has its way of living day to day. This is a story about how even though we may be alike in many ways, there are different rules and ways of living.

Aura was with her cousin. They had set up a kind of cab with two seats, one behind the other; she was the passenger, and Diego, her cousin, was the driver.

-Where am I taking her? -He asked seriously.

-To the toy store at the mall, tonight I'll be there playing and testing all the toys; that's my job.

-Envious, aren't they looking for new employees?

-No, it's only for girls.

-What a pity.

Her cousin drove down the road that would take her to the mall. Aura got off gracefully and went to the toy store, which was a pile of toys of them littering the floor.

Aura felt hungry and went to the kitchen; she saw a large jar with wrapped candy next to the refrigerator. She took one out and ate it. It was very sweet and sticky, and then she enjoyed licking each of her fingers.

-What did you do?

-I ate this candy; it was delicious.

-We have to ask permission to eat those and anything else. You can't just take it like that. His cousin looked very serious.

-I'm sorry, I didn't know.

Aura was visiting her cousin Diego's house, and she would stay there for several days. It was the first time she visited them and was left alone.

-At home, I eat what I want when I want, she added; that's why I thought I could.

-We have to tell them what you did. There's nothing wrong with that. They're not going to be mad.

Aura didn't feel comfortable with herself. She didn't like to look bad in other houses. So, they both went and found Diego's parents in the living room, each reading a book.

-Aura ate a piece of candy from the kitchen without asking for it first.

She felt bad for such a direct accusation. Diego didn't mean it in the wrong way, though.

-I understand, said his mother.

-But she didn't know the rules of this house.

-I see. -She looked at Aura. Are you hungry, honey? -She said as she stroked her head.

-I only ate one. I didn't know.

-Don't worry, we don't usually eat between meals. We want to make sure Diego eats everything when we serve him. So don't worry; you know you have to ask first or wait for us to give them to him.

Aura felt a little better.

-What other rules do you have?

Aura wanted to make sure she behaved well in the house.

Diego looked at her and then answered.

-I don't know, I go to bed at 7 p.m.

-I go to bed at 8.

-I have to brush and floss before I go to bed.

-Me too.

-I can't leave toys lying around. If I use them, I put them away.

-Me, not so much when mom reminds me, I do.

While they were talking about what they were doing

in each house, Aura moved to explain how they had the bed set up and accidentally touched a bureau. On it, there was a porcelain of a child looking at the sky. It wobbled and fell, breaking into several pieces.

Aura was frightened and saw her cousin and this in the direction of her mother.

She reacted and got down on her knees to pick everything up.

-I'm so sorry, Aura said as she piled up the pieces, trying to put them back together.

-Don't worry. Things break sometimes.

-Everything is all right here? -Said the father, who showed up to see what was going on.

The mother told him what had happened, and far from getting angry, he said.

-It's nothing, children; go outside, so you don't cut yourselves while mom and I clean up.

Aura felt guilty about what happened. She cried even though she didn't want to.

-I'm so sorry, she said.

-You can't always be perfect. There are accidents that happen, don't worry about it. We love you very much, and if it broke, then it broke, it was an ornament, and that's it; we'll put another one, and that's it.

-We are not angry, said the mother, so don't worry anymore.

The mother hugged Aura and kissed her.

-You can always come, and if something happens, well, that's it. It's not a bad thing to die for.

Aura was very relieved. It had been a mistake, but she had learned from it. So they went to the living room to play cab again, only this time they added that they were from an application where she asked for it, and he would arrive soon after to pick her up.

Accidents can happen at any time. It's just a matter of accepting it and moving on because Aura has learned that each house has its own rules, and she must abide by them because she is in a home that is not hers, just as it could happen if they visited her.

Aura kept asking her cousin what the rules were, for example, when they ate, they stopped for a moment to bless the table, they held hands sometimes, and sometimes they didn't. At her house, what they did was that each one said thank you for the food they were going to eat.

At her house, what they did was that each one said thank you for the food they were going to eat.

In addition, she knew that she had time to watch television, but at home, she could spend the day enjoying herself.

She accepted each of the rules willingly and enjoyed the home environment they had where everyone communicated. She understood that having rules were helpful for each of the members to know their roles, rights, and responsibilities.

But what stayed in her mind the most was that nothing mattered even though they were cousins and very close. Every home has its rules, and they must respect them because it is part of their love for others, the respect for their own cultures.

When she returned home, she wished she could go back, she asked her parents to take her back soon, because even though there were accidents, even though she ate what she shouldn't have, the rest of the time they had a good time. The place where the figure she broke now had a beautiful owl that seemed to see her every time she passed.

-It's the animal of wisdom, said Diego's father. I've always loved them, so seriously, they look like the grandparents of all the little birds.

Aura learned that she could make mistakes but learn from them, no matter what might happen.

Remember that every house has its rules, and it's a good lesson to respect them. Not all families are like yours. That doesn't make them better or worse. They are different. Learn to respect and ask for the rules when you go to visit. It is a sign of love you have for them, and you will avoid doing something that will make you look bad.

Unconditional Love for Animals

Do you love animals? Have you ever wanted to take care of other living beings? Do you overthink what might happen in the future? This story is full of love for animals and the teaching to stop worrying so much about what might happen.

Lucy was a little girl who loved animals very much. So, for her, seeing a bunny, a dog, a bird, or any animal was a reason to feel immensely happy because she felt that they were the sweetest beings in the world. She wanted to hug them, caress them, and talk to them.

Sometimes when she saw a dog in the street, she would ask its owner for permission, and then she would pet it. Her noble soul made all the animals come to her and let her pet them, and they would do the same, whether it was the dogs licking her, the cats rubbing on her legs, or the birds watching her from a safe distance.

One day she was at home watching a program on the children's channel, the one she liked best. But there was something around her that made her lose her concentration. It was like a repeated noise that, over and over again, made her miss scenes from her program. Although, at first, she didn't know what it was, she soon turned off the TV and concentrated.

It was raining outside. Her city always had rain all around.

But soon after she managed to hear the noise, she knew what it was about.

She got up and tried to follow the noise, which was barely audible. It was very low. But as she walked, she began to hear it more and more intensely. She reached the front door and stuck her ear to it. She could hear it on the other side.

She opened it carefully and saw her garden, where her mother had flowers, medicinal plants, and a series of beautiful plants of many colors. That's where the sound she now heard came from.

She saw some leaves move and stepped back. Her father had warned her to be careful with the snakes that could hide inside the plants, but she moved them gently and looked because she already recognized the sound.

Behind an aloe plant stood, like a little ball of fur, frightened, a small, completely wet kitten that looked at her frightened and meowed surely at its mother.

Quickly she picked up the cat and took it inside, ran to the back room, took a towel she had especially for these cases, and wrapped the little animal that, although it looked scared at first, now seemed to be grateful for the warmth and stayed still.

-Don't be afraid, kitty, I'll take care of you.

The cat saw her and meowed.

-Are you hungry? I'll get you some milk.

She went to the kitchen, and there was her mother, who at first was surprised by the animal she brought with her, but she already knew her daughter. She rescued any animal she came across.

-Another one of your patients?

-He was in the garden.

-Poor thing, let's give him some milk.

-Yes, that's what I was coming to.

The mother helped him warm it up a bit and put it on him, and the cat immediately began to lick. He was hungry.

The cat spent that day very much at ease. First, Lucy played with him, and soon the little animal felt confident with the help of a rope and a ball tied on end. They had hours of fun.

That night, when her father arrived, mom told him about the new guest, and he showed up in her room to meet him.

-Hi, daddy said Lucy.

-Hi, little one. I see you have a guest.

-Yes, he's beautiful.

She told him what had happened and how she would take care of him until he had a new home. Lucy loved all animals, but cats were her favorite. She had never had the opportunity to adopt one, only to help them while their owner appeared or while she found a home for him.

-Would you like to adopt him? -asked her father.

Lucy's eyes sparkled with joy.

-Really?

He nodded.

-Although if the owners show up, we'll have to give him up.

Lucy accepted the proposal, although, in her eyes, there was a slight shadow of sadness.

Lucy decided to name the cat Pellet because when she saw him, he looked like a little ball of fur, only wet, but now, when he slept, he turned into a fluffy ball that she caressed for hours.

But having saved Pellet, she now felt a great fear that the cat's owners would show up, for no doubt he had not been born that long and the mother cat would be sad for him, or there would be a child missing him. This began to eat away at Lucy's mind. Although she enjoyed Pellet, she was always thinking if this would be their last day together.

Time went by, and that scared and wet kitten in the garden had now become a big cat with the look of a king who slept wherever he felt sleepy.

Lucy always loved her cat because, besides being hers, he was unique. His all-white color was only distinguished by a heart spot on his back, which, although barely visible when he was small, was now more marked. Her cat was unique.

This also caused him a bit of fear because that spot could be what was necessary for the real owner to identify him.

One thing the family liked to do was to go to a nearby mountain on Sundays. So after Pellet's arrival, he also went climbing the mountain. Lucy would put him in a special transparent backpack with holes for him to breathe, put him on her back, and they would go to the mountain, although Pellet would mostly sleep.

On one of these trips, a man kept seeing Lucy, especially her backpack with Pellet.

He seemed hesitant, but then he became animated and walked up to her, who was with her parents, and after swallowing his breath a couple of times, he spoke:

-Hello friends, good morning -he told them.

-Good morning, neighbor. -Said the father, who lived in the area.

-I think they have my cat.

The dreaded day had arrived for Lucy. For now, she would have to return to Pellet.

-Well, said the father, we've had him for quite a while. Are you sure he's yours?

-That spot on his back is unique. One day I left the door open by accident and never found him again. I'm glad he's okay, and he looks well cared for and full of love. -Turning to Lucy, Do you love my cat very much?

Lucy nodded, thinking full of terror that the next thing that man would do would be to open the bag and take Pellet. Such was her fear that she felt her eyes burning and tears welling up.

-Don't be like that, the man hastened to say, I see you have the cat well taken care of, and I see him very peaceful. I think he is in the right place. You have had him longer than me. Now he is more yours than mine. I only ask you one thing, fill him with lots of love.

The man turned his back and left. He turned around and waved goodbye. That was the happiest day for Lucy. The anguish for the owner to appear and take the cat away was over.

She realized that for a long time, she had thought about losing Pellet, and everything turned out better than expected.

Lucy learned that giving love has good results. She had a living being that followed her around the house. When she had a cold or felt terrible, he was by her side, loyal to her, and that anxiety and fear only increased something that, in the end, turned out better.

Don't think so much about tomorrow because

things will turn out differently than you fear, and you love animals very much. They are noble beings and willing to love you if you let them.

Day with Grandma

Do you have someone you admire? Do you long to do something amazing? When you get to know those loved ones better, you discover a universe in the things they do. The moments you spend together will be unforgettable. That is precisely what this story is about.

For Diana, her grandmother was the most special person in the world. She loved her with all her heart and enjoyed every moment they shared to the fullest.

She was an exceptional woman, a sculptor, she would take a piece of deformed rock, and with chisel and hammer, she would sculpt incredible figures. She said she felt she was like a modern-day Michelangelo.

Diana loved a figure she had in her house. It was a baby turtle with the sweetest face she had ever seen.

She was going to go visit her after a while, and this made her very excited.

Dear and beloved granddaughter, how good it is to see you! -Diana also let herself be squeezed and kissed only by her grandmother. With the others, she wiped the kiss with the back of her hand.

-I wanted to see you, grandmother.

-I wanted to see you, and today I have a big surprise for you.

Although grandmother made the sculptures using chisels and hammers, she used them to carve shapes and details, but she used machines to polish the stone to cut large pieces. She had to make cuts and then start detailing.

Grandmother and granddaughter set off for the

workshop as she said to him:

-I know new adventures can be scary, but if you don't live them, you don't learn things. As long as what you do doesn't pose a danger, it's okay to venture.

They reached the huge door leading to the workshop that she had so far seen from the outside, Grandma took off the padlock and when she was about to open it, Diana said:

-Give me a moment, Grandma. I need to get used to the idea.

-Do you want me to shake my hand to make you feel better?

Diana shook her head. She motioned to her, and Grandma opened the door.

As soon as she entered, she felt immense anxiety come over her as if something was consuming her inside and her feet had stuck to the floor. She began to see all the space inside, it was very dark, and her sight was not yet adapted to the sunlight outside with the darkness inside.

She began to see figures, first that of a huge witch with a wide dress, then she saw that it was only a covered sculpture.

Then she saw a kind of trident that was going to come at her to pierce her, but she realized that it was only a rake. Thus she saw many figures.

-Grandmother.

-Here I am, go ahead and I'll wait for you.

The grandmother was in the back. She had passed in front of Diana and was beginning to do her business.

The view adapted to the interior. She found chisels of all kinds, brushes of all sizes, strange machines she did not know, and dust, lots of rock dust from the many pieces Grandma had built.

Grandma was waiting for her at the end, ready to show her things. There was a large lamp and a sculpture halfway at work.

-This is my special place, where I forget the world exists and get to do a thousand things.

-It's... unique. -said Diana.

-I see you noticed all the tools. Another day I'll show you what each one does.

-Now, I want you to take that chisel and that hammer. I have prepared a small rock for you to learn how to sculpt.

Diana looked around. It was a messy place, but at the same time, very nice and cozy. Some windows overlooked a courtyard that had many plants, her grandmother loved flowers and plants, and she took great care of them. Tables everywhere, tools left to chance. But for some reason, she felt very good there.

The stone she had for herself was the size of a soccer, so she could do a medium-sized job. According to her grandmother, it would make a sculpture almost 20 cm high. She showed her an elementary design of a kitten.

-You'll start with the basics, don't be afraid to make a mistake. -She told her.

She showed her some gloves that she put on, and they seemed rough; her hands were limited, but when she picked up the chisel, it seemed that she could not hold it. Grandmother told her that she would not get hurt by those.

-This is the big chisel. It will be useful for you to do the first work. You will be able to cut the bigger pieces.

-When will I use the brushes?

-Those are for when we are giving the most advanced finishes, details like the eye, or where the rock is barely scraped to give aesthetics and shape.

-Should I hit with the hammer?

-Yes. Hug the chisel with your hand. Now, you will use the hammer to hit the chisel on the head, holding it tight.

Diana gave the first blow, and with a little fear, the rock was barely marked.

-You have to do it harder, but it's okay for that first try.

Diana dedicated herself to gently touching and tapping the rock. And then, with more confidence, she kept on picking at the rock until a piece of it fell to the ground.

-That's it! That's exactly what sculpting is, to begin to remove everything that's left over.

-I like what you're doing.

-Wait till you start shaping; you've barely taken a piece off. What do you think comes first?

-Do the ears?

-Exactly, we'll make the cat's ears. There where you cut, you can start forming a triangle; for that, take this smaller chisel and start carving.

Diana began to hit gently and saw how the rock dust was falling and was making a triangle somewhat deformed. She saw her grandmother, and she seemed to read her mind.

-Don't worry. We'll do the details later; right now, we'll just make the shape, like the silhouettes you make at school, and then fill in the whole figure.

-I understand.

-On the inner side of the ear, you will make the cat's head, which is half oval, and then you will make the other ear.

Grandmother explained to her how to place the chisel so that it would cut cleanly and make the rock take the shape she wanted. She made the other ear and then a round face that looked more like an alien than a cat.

You are doing it like an artist. If you work on the habit, I am sure in time, you will be able to create pieces like no other. You'll be a better sculptor than me.

Diana thought about how that cat might look at the end, when she carved it completely, she imagined painting it, making the fur with the tiny chisels, and getting her first work of art thanks to her grandmother's knowledge.

Grandmother and granddaughter spent the rest of the day carving the stone, then she watched as grandmother began with her art to masterfully carve and shape it as if she were molding plasticine instead of chopping rocks. She could not believe that her sweet grandmother could achieve that. She also felt happy to see her in her world, her universe. It seemed that the world outside had stopped.

Far away was that initial anxiety when she started to carve. She was happy to have gone to the workshop, and although she was a novice, she was sure that with practice, she would be able to carve any piece that crossed her mind.

When you share with people from other generations, like our grandparents, you open yourself to a universe of knowledge and new experiences. They know a lot, and the bond you make will never be forgotten.

Sick on Halloween

Have you ever looked forward to a day and suddenly got sick? Have you wanted to do something and then plans to fall through? Do you find it hard to forgive? This story, full of great adventures, will teach you how beautiful it can be to share with those who have less and that, many times, anger only pushes people away.

Dana and her younger brother, Lucas, got along well. Still, like all siblings, they sometimes fought over playful situations that ended with both of them sulking in some corner of the house. Still, despite everything, they always made plans for great adventures.

What they had most on their minds during these times was the approaching Halloween, and it was already a tradition for them to go out with a big bag each to play at every house and shout:

-Sweet or trick - and from inside, they would give them different candies that they would happily take, and then their mother would administer them to them so they wouldn't eat it all on the first night.

What they were doing these last few days was planning how they would enjoy the day. Lucas had prepared a costume of his favorite superhero, one that flew and had a red metallic suit that had many weapons and faced the bad guys.

Dana had prepared the costume of a princess she loved to see on TV with long, straight hair. They had both tried on their costumes and loved them.

It was three days before Halloween, and all they could talk about was Halloween.

-Since I'm a princess, I'm going to get more candy than you, said Dana arrogantly.

-Well, since I'm a superhero, I'll get more. If not, she raised a hand and pretended to shoot; I'll pulverize them with my gamma ray.

-What, ray, you're not the superhero. You're just in disguise.

-And you're not a princess, you're just in disguise, you're a normal girl.

Dana opened her eyes wide and looked at her brother with annoyance. She got up and left him alone.

She considered herself quite the princess; her mother always told her she was a beautiful princess when she did her hair. She could not believe what Lucas had just told her.

-He was just playing, her mother told her when he told her. Besides, he told me that you told him he wasn't a superhero.

-But he's not!

-But he's excited about being one.

Dana didn't understand or didn't want to. She felt hurt by her brother and more so because he didn't seem to care or had already forgotten she had said it.

The night before Halloween, Dana felt a stitch in her head; for one thing, it was unusual for her to be in pain. She told her mother, and she gave her some pink syrup that tasted horrible and took her temperature.

Lucas started to feel sick too, not a headache, but his eyes.

-What do you feel? -His mother said

-I feel like my whole eye hurts, and on top of that, my forehead hurts a little.

Soon after, they both had a fever, not very high, but enough to make them feel sick, and Mom imposed a regimen of a series of medications and complete rest.

-But tomorrow is Halloween. -Dana said.

-Let's hope they'll have a better day tomorrow. -Mom said.

That night they slept badly; they woke up cold and hot, with a general malaise of all kinds, and their mother gave them medicines. At dawn, they both felt bad, still feeling sick.

Mom called the doctor, who came to the house and checked them out, ruling that it was something viral and that, with some medicine, they would get over it.

It was nothing serious; the only terrible thing was that they would have to rest, and no way they would be able to sleep at night, warm, at home, and quiet so that they would heal soon.

-But today is Halloween, said Dana.

-I'm sorry, you won't be able to go out, said the doctor; next year it will be.

Both Lucas and Dana felt terrible, not because of the discomfort, but because what they had planned so much had been ruined.

Almost at nightfall, their mother suggested they dress up to be ready to enjoy that night so that despite everything, it was Halloween, and inside the house, they could have fun.

Neither of them wanted to.

-We can play Halloween. I'll lock myself in the room, you play in costume, and when you open the door. I'll give you candy. -The mother proposed.

The children did not accept. They thought it was boring.

What they did do was stand at the window of the house to see their neighbors going from house to house, knocking and asking for candy. They passed by their home several times and asked why they did not go out. Mom answered everyone that because they felt terrible, they had to rest.

They saw neighbors dressed as vampires, others as ghosts, a little boy dressed as a bear, and so on; one by one, they saw princesses and zombies, knights' spears, and superheroes. Some were in simpler costumes, all having fun outside, while the two of them stood there, bored, even though mom was trying hard to entertain them because she seemed to feel sad that her children were missing the day they had planned so much.

The ones Dana and Lucas saw often were the Jones brothers. Four almost teenage brothers who had the costume of a crazy family, all with ugly clothes, scarred faces, and a fake axe on their backs, would knock on the door, scream like crazy, and from inside, they would laugh and give them more candy. They each had a pillowcase, and it was almost full of stuff.

When they knocked on Dana and Lucas', they were quite affected by the siblings' luck of not being able to leave due to illness.

As they were leaving, they waved goodbye as they saw them at the window; Dana and Lucas did the same with long faces.

That night, when everything was calming down and almost no children were knocking on the door, the Jones brothers arrived at Dana and Lucas' door.

-Didn't they already come here? -Dana said.

-Maybe they want more candy.

-But they can't fit anything in their bags.

They knocked on the door, and the mother opened it.

-We know Dana and Lucas are sick; that's why we brought you this. -Said the older brother.

They handed over two pillowcases, one for each of them.

-They are very good, said the mother. -Come, thank your friends who brought you these.

They each received a bag and thanked her. Suddenly they both felt better; that kind gesture had filled their souls.

The brothers left, and Dana and Lucas could not believe it; the ones who had collected the most stuff that day had given half of the loot to them.

-That's called nobility and solidarity. So you see, children, said mom.

Lucas asked permission to eat something, and the mother left them a sweet for each until they were healed. It was a great booty. There was everything; they chose a gummy she and a bonbon he. They both enjoyed it.

Dana watching her brother eat and thinking about the Jones, felt she was upset for nothing with her brother; it had been a spur-of-the-moment thing. Besides, she thought about her neighbors; they were good and how giving when another is bad did a great deed.

Sometimes Dana can get upset, but letting that stay in the heart is not good; giving when another is in need is great to work that can even almost cure you of an illness.

Learn to give a little to those who don't have and don't hold grudges in your heart; you often feel angry and don't even remember why. It is better to love.

Bad Moods

Are there days when you feel like you're in a bad mood? Do you feel like you can't stand anything? Are these feelings making you feel bad? Don't push away what you think. It's an excellent time to remember how much you love yourself. In this story, you will learn that.

Rachel had had a bad night, one of those nights where she would wake up all night, tossing and turning and waking up out of nowhere. Now when she had to get ready for school, her head was spinning, her eyes were heavy, and the last thing she wanted to do was get out of bed.

-Rachel, love, you have to go to school; come on, get up. -Her mother told her.

-I don't want to go anywhere, she said moodily.

-Are you all right? Are you feeling sick?

-I slept badly; I woke up a lot.

-I'm sorry, that's bad. But you can't skip school, come on, get up and go to school, and when you come back, you take a nap.

Rachel sat up from bed and made a bad face; she was very upset, with herself, with her mom waking her up, with school and her schedule. Her mom gave her the shirt to put on, her clothes, the dress, and the whole uniform for school.

Her clothes were too tight this morning, the buttons on her shirt felt like metal nails, her dress felt rough, and her shoes felt smaller than usual, her socks seemed to choke her feet, and her hair seemed more tangled than ever.

On her way out, she stumbled and felt angry; everything was going wrong for her that morning. As she reached the kitchen for the breakfast that Mom was preparing for her, she saw with annoyance what she was doing. Mom put the plate of food on the table for her.

Rachel looked at the plate and saw her mom in annoyance. She wrinkled her mouth and put her arms across her chest, crossed, locked in her annoyance.

-You should eat a little before you go. Then you can feel better, go on, and eat.

-I don't want to.

The mother sighed and said in a sweet tone:

-If you want to be grumpy, the only person you're hurting is yourself.

Rachel pouted and wrinkled her face even more, she tightened her arms and knew that what her mother said was true, but now it seemed that she didn't want anything else.

Her mother hugged her, gave her some food, and showered her with kisses, this calmed her down a little, and mom said:

-I love you very much, my daughter.

-I love you too, Mom.

The two hugged each other, and she realized that she felt better, that this hug filled with so much love calmed her down.

This is the best gift you can have, to fill yourself with love so you can feel better.

Rachel felt good. She even felt like smiling. She ate everything and left for school to be on time.

That day was on the court with her friends, the bad mood was gone, and she didn't even feel sleepy, although her eyes were a little heavy. She had smiled all morning as she did every day. She was like this, thanks to his mother's loving embrace.

Mom had said nice things to her, and she felt she should pass that message on to someone else. Help anyone he might need. She looked around at all her friends and noticed Peter sitting apart, separate from the others. Usually, he was very happy and was the soul of the group, but now he was very quiet. He looked angry. He was looking at a notebook and seemed very upset.

-Is everything all right? -She asked.

-No. He looked annoyed. He didn't want to talk to anyone, he avoided her gaze.

-Do you want to talk about it?

-No.

-I'll stand here if you need anything.

She didn't want to push anyone to do something he wasn't comfortable with. Especially when he wasn't in a good mood, she didn't like being approached. So she wouldn't do it to others.

She gave him his space, but kept a sly eye on him, saw him stand up at one point and throw a notebook over a wall in annoyance. Finally, she realized that even if he wanted to be alone, he needed someone to give him a hand, so she got up and went to look for him. After approaching, she stood at a safe distance.

-What are you doing? -He asked her.

-I wanted you to know that you're not alone, even if

you're like this.

Peter crossed his arms and made a face.

-I don't want you near me.

-I know, I understand, I was like that this morning, but when we're like this is when we need others the most.

-That's the dumbest thing you've said since I've known you.

-All right, I understand, as I said, but I'm here if you want to talk. Whenever you want to come.

He answered nothing, snorted, and turned his back on her.

Rachel sat aside, and he started playing with a Rubik's cube, trying to solve it. She didn't come over to him as she promised. Then they had to go to class, and they all left where they were.

Later she noticed that Peter was in a better mood. Although he didn't look quite right, he was calmer.

-Do you want a hug? -She said as she approached him.

He looked at her for a few seconds and then answered as if pretending to be unconcerned.

-Well, if you want.

Rachel hugged him affectionately.

-I hope you have the best day tomorrow and have a good time, have a good day tomorrow and always.

After this, they left each one for home. The weekend was coming, and they did not see each other until Monday. When they met again, Peter approached her and greeted her.

-Hello Peter, how did you have a good time this weekend?

-Better, fine, thank you, I had a good time.

He smiled with much affection. He looked good and cheerful. He had an almost angelic smile, and his teeth were fully visible.

-It's great that you're better.

-I wanted to apologize for what happened the other day. I felt terrible because I thought I treated you the wrong way.

-Don't worry, we have days like that, sometimes we get angry and do bad things, but kindness is the best antidote, I'm glad it helped.

-I didn't mean what I said anyway. I was in a bad mood.

-It's part of being a good friend; even when you yelled at me, it was nice to have helped you. I didn't know I wanted to hug you, either. I helped you.

-Thanks for what you did.

-I'm glad I could help you. I'm glad the hugs made you feel better.

- I was really surprised that I could feel better after you hugged me and left.

-It was nothing. Thank you for coming to say this. It makes my day to have done something good with you.

You can learn to be kind and empathetic to others because you will never know when you need help.

That you put the needs of others before your own allows you to think outside of yourself and keeps your heart open to kindness.

The people who love us and whom we love will teach us amazing ways to improve ourselves and inspire us to achieve amazing things.

Exhausted Mom

Have you ever stopped to think about how hard your mom works? Do you know that she puts in a lot of effort? Our parents make many efforts and sacrifices, so everything at home runs smoothly. This story is a vivid example of that.

Sophia and Isabella were two sisters who were a year apart; they usually spent the year with half a day at school, and when they got home, a good part of the afternoon studying and preparing for the other day. Although vacation times were somewhat boring, the two shared the day at home, playing games, watching movies, and playing a console, lengthening the hours of solitude they both had to endure. There were days when there was a nanny, but they did not like it very much because she put them to do homework, wash dishes, pick up the mess and even sweep. On the other hand, when they were alone, they did not have to do anything. They just had to enjoy themselves or wait for the time to pass until mom came home from work in the afternoon.

Both sisters woke up early for a moment when their mother would come and give them each a kiss on the forehead and always told them the same thing.

-You behave well, try not to make too much of a mess, and remember, you play with one thing, put it away, and move on to something else.

They both nodded their heads and turned over to continue sleeping. Between dreams they listened to the instructions, the meals were in the refrigerator, they had to heat it, to call her by video call when they woke up, to write, not to neglect the cell phone so they could contact them when she had time.

They both answered with a nagging:

-Yes, mom.

When Sophia and Isabella got up, they walked around the house, looked for food, ate breakfast, and cleaned themselves. One of them got on the phone, and the other turned on the TV. When Sophia finished eating, she left her plate on the table, Isabella left the paper roll with a long strip on the floor and the towel to dry her hands on the floor when she left the bathroom.

The lights in the bedrooms were on. The microwave door was open, with the light reflecting off one wall.

The mother called by video call, and Sophia answered:

-Hi, daughter; where's Isabella?

-Over there.

-Call her to talk.

-Isabella!

At once, she came up and showed herself on camera, waving her hand in greeting.

-Did they eat? -asked the mother.

They both nodded.

-Did you have the lights on in the rooms?

They both looked at each other, and Isabella went to turn them off after smiling.

-Please, turn off the lights, it's to take care of the planet and my pocket too, electricity is expensive.

-Yes, mom, said Sophia.

-What is that light?

Sophia moved the camera in the direction shown by her mother, and it was the microwave.

-Close that microwave door immediately.

Sophia got up and closed it.

-They just got up, and already the house is upside down; please, be tidier. I'm tired of so much work, daughters, help me. I barely have enough strength to prepare things for the next day.

-Okay, said Isabella, who was already in front of the camera again.

Mom gave them other indications and said she would call them again after lunch. She had to work.

Sophia suggested to Isabella that they play in the room; they went in, opened the toy closet, and took out everything, a giant cloth bag full of many things, from baby maracas to stuffed animals that they hadn't seen for a long time. They made a river of stuff on the floor and entertained themselves for about 15 minutes.

Then Sophia suggested they watch a kitten app she had downloaded the night before, and there they were given lunchtime.

That's how they went through the day. In every room they went through, they left a mess; they played ghosts with the blankets on the beds and then left around the sheets and pillows, everything, the bare mattress in the room.

That afternoon when Mom returned, as soon as she walked through the door, she found a house that looked like it had been hit by a hurricane, everything upside down, the living room furniture cushions on the floor, the dishes from the day's meal accumulating flies, the refrigerator half open with the light coming through the crack, the bedrooms with everything on the floor, the bathroom with the lid up and a mess of products.

-Girls! -was the mother's way of showing how upset she was.

They both appeared to greet her with joy, but the smile they were wearing disappeared when they saw the mother's face.

-What did I tell you earlier?

They both remained silent, searching for the answer.

-To have order in the house! Look how you have everything, now besides doing everything I have to do, I will also have to tidy up this house because you were incapable.

The mother made a strange grimace and went to her room.

Both sisters looked at each other with guilty faces and walked almost noiselessly, peeking into the room.

Mom was sitting on the edge of the mattress, on the bed, with her hands. She was holding her head, frustrated. She looked terrible like she was trying to deal with a lot of things.

Sophia motioned for her sister to follow her, and they both went into the living room.

-I think we messed up, Sophia said.

-Yes, we made a bit of a mess.

-We have to do something, let's tidy up now, and when mom comes out, she can see things in order and be happy, okay?

The other nodded, and they immediately started tidying up.

Soon after, they had washed the dishes, tidied up the bathroom, and picked up every single toy in the room, it wasn't perfect, but at least they had evened it out a bit. The beds were poorly laid out, but it was just a matter of mom smoothing it out, and it was ready.

When mom came out, already resigned to the fact that she would have to get down to work to tidy everything up, she was surprised to see that the house was tidier.

She saw the girls looking guilty and waiting for her

reaction. The mother knelt to be at their level and told them to come closer, to hug them.

The three of them gave each other a long hug, and then she gently pulled them aside to speak to them.

-I understand that you want to play, and that's fine; I like you to have fun, but it doesn't cost you anything to tidy up a little. How long did it take you to organize what you did just now? Nothing, just a little while; I spend all day at work, it takes me an hour to go, an hour to come back, I prepare your lunch for tomorrow, mine, I tidy up things at home when I go to do the shopping, it takes more hours, I wish it wasn't like that, but it's hopeless, it's what we have to do. Thank you for helping me to tidy up.

The three of them hugged each other, and from that day on, they began to play with things and tidy them up. In the evenings, when mom came home, instead of each one staying in her own space, they would help her with something or at least keep her company, tell her things, and even complain about each other, just like any other family.

Our parents go out of their way to get things done. Sophia and Isabella learned this from seeing their mom exhausted from picking up messes.

It's okay to play like any other child, but for every mess you make, pick it up and support your parents; they go out of their way to ensure you are comfortable and don't miss anything.

Two Languages

Are you afraid of what people will say about your culture? Do you think you are not part of a group even if you haven't shown what makes you stand out? This story shows how the world is full of cultures and can open you up to meeting more people.

Arya was getting ready to go to class. She was

nervous and felt like she had butterflies in her stomach. It wasn't new what she was feeling, but it bothered her a lot. Every day at home, she felt comfortable, but when she left, it gave her a feeling of sadness, as if she was leaving something of herself behind. In a way, it was like that.

She spoke two languages, English and Hindi, by inheritance from her father, who was from India.

She knew that her classmates did not understand her language at school, so when she was with them, she felt she could not be herself.

-Alavida- said by way of farewell as she was leaving the house. She was saying goodbye to her mother and grandmother. Then, she walked out and down the driveway.

Once at school, after chatting with some friends, she waited for her class to start.

-Hi, Arya - said Matilda, her best friend. She sat next to her in the classroom.

Arya smiled softly at her and said,

-Hi.

Arya liked Matilda. She was a sweet and kind girl. She had short shoulder-length dark black hair, very different from hers, which was thicker and a little longer.

Matilda liked to sit next to Arya, as they talked a lot, and in the off hours, they would play games or talk about anything. This was something Arya always appreciated.

At the beginning of class, Arya settled into her seat and watched the others answer various questions they were asking about the subjects. Although she knew the answers to almost everything, she didn't feel comfortable participating.

When the teacher finished the lineup of questions, she handed out a test. Arya saw that it was something about math. She knew quite a bit about the subject, but she felt nervous, anxiety began to quicken her breathing, and she began to feel a little choked up.

Arya took out the pencil case, and because she was so anxious, when she tried to open it, it slipped out of her hands and fell to the floor. The pencils began to roll like little cylinders lying down, and the crash of the wood on the floor made the whole room look at her.

Every one of her classmates turned to look at her, and Arya felt her face burning. She looked down and whispered:

-Mujhe Maaf Karen (I'm sorry).

She started to pick everything up quickly and felt someone tap her on the shoulder. She turned and saw:

-Shall I help you?

It was her friend who wanted to help her.

-Yes, you are very kind, she said.

They quickly picked up the things and put them in the pencil case and the bag.

-What was that you said when you dropped your things? -she asked her later.

Arya did a little memory recall and said she had felt it. Then she felt sorry, she hadn't thought that others had heard her, and then she said:

-My father is from India, and we have a lot of his

culture; we speak Hindi at home. It's something I say when I feel a little sorry. I say sorry to apologize.

-That's great, said Matilda.

The teacher announced that they were now back to the test. They had already picked up all the mess.

-I'm sorry, teacher, said both girls. They finished putting things away and sat down in their seats.

-I want to know more about that language you speak, said Matilda.

-We talked about it at lunch.

Arya felt pride and surprise. She didn't think other people, not even Matilda, would be interested in knowing about her culture.

When they finished eating, both friends sat down on a bench in the small school playground, and Arya looked to the side. Almost the whole room was watching her.

A boy who had never spoken to her before said to her a little shyly:

-Matilda said that you could tell us about your other

language, that thing you said in class.

Arya looked at her friend, winked, and gave him a thumbs up, amused.

-I think it's great that you're speaking more languages. -said another boy.

-Several of them are interested in learning more about you since they have never met anyone who speaks other languages.

They all seemed excited to meet her.

Arya was surprised that so many people wanted to know more about her language and that she could tell them anecdotes or whatever. They all looked at her with curiosity and in a friendly manner. She realized that she had practically never spoken to them before.

Now she felt a little embarrassed, and she blushed, for it was not comfortable to be the center of attention. Matilda stood next to her and smiled at her to encourage her. She said to her:

-You don't have to; it's not obligatory. But I think you are special and everyone wants to know more.

Arya thought about it some more, sighed deeply, and then said, Okay:

-Okay. What do they want to know?

So, each child began to speak at a time, and she asked them one at a time, then they began:

-Water.

-Paanee

-Sweets

-Meetha

-Cold

-Sardee.

So, one by one, they asked her words that she answered. At the end, a girl asked her:

-How is it that you speak two languages and especially that rare language?

-My family came to this country years ago, specifically my dad, and at home, we grew up with Indian culture. They helped me learn English and Hindi. I even speak a little Spanish.

Everyone was shocked that she spoke all those languages.

-How many languages are there in the world? -asked one child.

Another boy, who was very astonished and apparently from another classroom, looked at her and asked her many questions.

Arya thought the question was a very good one. She had never stopped to think about how many languages there were in the world. She saw Matilda, and she was smiling very sweetly. Maybe she had always known that Arya wasn't happy without showing some of who she was. Her culture, her language. It was no longer a secret, and the heartfelt more relieved to be rid of that weight.

Arya set about explaining to everyone what things meant, how it was part of the culture, and that the letters were not the same as the alphabet they knew but others that would surely look like scribbles to her.

She wrote some things down for them, and everyone was surprised that they now had more questions. Arya felt very comfortable chatting with her friends and showing the Hindu part of her life. She was grateful to Matilda for helping her take that step she had held back so much before. Arya approached her friend, hugged her, and said shukriya.

-What does that mean?

-Thank you. You are a great friend.

-You are too, and I love sharing with you.

-And me.

-Will you teach me how to speak Hindi?

-Of course, you have to work hard because it's a complex language.

-I'm sure if you teach it to me, it won't be so hard.

Arya already knew that many people appreciated her for who she was and how she showed her way of being. She felt happier.

She wanted to go home and tell her family what she had experienced that day. It was wonderful to speak two languages.

You have to be comfortable with who you are, learn to be yourself, and love yourself fully. Try to see beyond what people believe and expect of you. You may be surprised to discover that you were wrong about what others thought. You may enter a wonderful world full of great experiences where you will grow and learn new things.

Learn to embrace your culture and don't be afraid or ashamed to show it to the world; the world is full of many cultures and ways of being

Made in United States
North Haven, CT
19 April 2024

51533811R00055